The Look of Beauty

– POEMS BY PAUL H. SIMMONS –

http://www.fast-print.net/bookshop

THE LOOK OF BEAUTY

A catalogue record for this book is available from the British Library

ISBN 978-178456-267-0

First published 2015 by
FASTPRINT PUBLISHING
Peterborough, England.

For Isobel and Freddie

Contents

Mona Lisa

So it really is enigma,
That mystery in a smile,
A gentle touch of kindness,
To comfort or beguile.
The darkness mellows quietly;
The hair is neatly kept,
But on her chest shines lightness,
Below a shaded neck.

The hands are pure and natural,
The clothes are plain and staid,
But on her arms there's richness,
Round the shoulder there's a drape.
It seems she has serenity; authority - so blessed;
She seems to come from gentle climes,
Those eyes are fine and wise.

She rests like some strange vanguard,
A type or figurehead,
With paths to sea behind her
And look stretched far ahead.
A trace of veil on her plain hair;
Beauty from each side;
Her mind a happy, half-closed book,
And little sign of virgin
In that subtle, knowing look.

Communication

Some things I know without a word,
They dwell where no man's been;
But in the everyday exchange
We see confusion reign.

Tripartite talk is trite and short - perhaps a third is
lost...
Our looks engage in one-to-one,
But often truth is spun.
And when we aim to deal in facts
Then we still forget,
To teach, remind and interact,
And so the trap is set.

We speak too soft, too loud, too late;
Does this communicate?
And every truth that we evade
It ceases to explain.

When admonition turns awry
and patient talk is gone;
When commentators lose respect
and interviews go wrong;

Or ranting at our neighbour (sure, you never do),
But have you ever thrown away a word,
Not one; then maybe two?

These are then the words that hurt,
The wrongs that drag us down,
Or memories from childhood
When friends are lost and found.

Speak to each with gentleness,
Just like a common prayer,
And heed the present, and the past,
When you are talking there;
For you will still remember
Some voices like a curse;
And lips can even shatter
A fragile, carefree verse.

Dilettante

Your choice is just to pick a life,
To do a little here;
To see a little there;
Delight, imagine, tales and yarns,
Without the lion's share.

Glory in another's fame,
But never front of stage,
Always picking your way through
Those sunny summer days.

When winter lays its hand on you
You quiver to the bone;
Your sprightly summer dance is fled,
Your gaiety is gone.

Another day, another game
Is set to entertain,
But you must wait, anticipate,
The taste of things to come.

But then it falters, can't be found,
This overwhelming joy;

Just like the scholars deeply set,
Whose knowledge seems to cloy.

A bad start in life

Where we start is commonplace, where we've been is
wild;
From the land of spirits is born a starving child.
Every little detail, every road we tread,
Remember from the ecstasy, like a moment's death.
Before that the brooding, after that what's bad,
For every start is troubled, poor or rich or glad.

In the dim beginning there was earth and sea;
At our dawn was circumstance, a certain place to be,
Weathered by discoveries, nothing if not free.

All with limitations, and with inner shame,
Curse the lot that they've been dealt,
Perhaps a pointless game.

Some in health and beauty, and radiance of face;
Others lost in vanity along the cat-walk race:
They have made a step in fame; or step into a dream;

Bad start is never how it looks, and luck's not what it
seems.

Heatwave

Bring on the heat, the sweat that cools,
The summer breeze and the English fools,
Who venture out with awkward tread,
And snow-white feet and furnace head.
Into the evening shade lead on,
Day has blistered, come and gone;
But heat burns on into the night,
As eyes eclipse the moon's delight.

Stay and fret into the morning,
Heady senses, thrashing, turning;
Until the warm, incessant sun
Warns us that new day's begun.

Enter then the next extreme -
Brightness blinds and light-fall gleams;
Dryness withers all that grows,
High roads melt, and seeds are blown.
In our minds with fevered hours
We long for water; spring-time showers.

Sun beats down and burnishes,
Times are spent in idleness;
A new creation now we crave
As we are wrought by pure heatwave.

Discipline

Perhaps a kind of virtue, but more an earthly claim;
It helps to edify a life, and counts encumbered days.

Such a crucial challenge, when in uniform we stand,
Proud to serve and cherish our sober, native land.

Here the tiresome treadmill, where we test our days,
Where the ordered times are set, and certain music
played.

But there the soul finds ample space, and unity within,
Where eternal freedom frees from discipline.

Good and Bad Strife

The games played out in olive groves, upon the
mountain sides.
They ran to end all marathons, they fought a
comrade's fight –
And all with restitution, all righteous was that fight.
In their flesh-bound orgy of writhing blood-sweat life
They also bred a love-match to drug impassioned
strife.

But then another sword or blow, a greater injury,
Revived a savage strife that killed, the depth of tragedy.
From the garden groves they're torn - into fiercest
storm.
So then where is the honour fled, and virtue with its
calm?
Where then the game of innocence, and all that simple
harm?

In a quiet room

As we shout and noise comes out, or mutter from afar;
Sit with strangers nervously as silence strains and jars.
Feel the clatter of our jaws when nonsense is
exchanged
With some sort of comedian whose act is purely
feigned.

Take the ranting world by storm, and never say a
word;
Meditate while we negate the turmoil on our own.
They can fidget, maybe fret - where is speech they say?
Without chatter where is man, throughout the livelong
day?

If only we could rest awhile, quite perfectly as still
As trees at night or tables decked with lowly daffodils.
Within a room just filled with scent and freshness of
the air,
Where we could sit and simply think, or sometimes
only stare.

"All men's miseries derive from not being able to sit in a quiet room alone."
Blaise Pascal

To take a risk

I think I will stay sometime upon the London roads;
That should be a risk enough,
To change employment, swap abodes.

My job shall be to honour the famous London tribes
Who sleep upon the pavement, washed up in London's
tide.

I'm always being told to take a fearless risk,
To exercise my inner life –
To steal that secret kiss.

So I will take myself to streets;
To those dirty little back streets,
Or to boxes by the bridge,
And I will delve in litter
As if my home-spun fridge.

And when I've taken every risk to body, mind and
more,
And there is little change upon the Thameside shore -
Do you know what then I'll do? –
I'll beg for that damn job back, the one I left before,
The one I lost so lightly, of which I was so sure.

But then I will be guided, politely, door to door,
Escorted from the back one, from whence I'm seen no
more.

E. & O. E.

If errors and omissions could all be blotted out,
What would there be left for the poor pen to write
    about?

Please accept apologies, please except, excuse,
Please excise, cut out our lies,
For without this we die.

Dependency

They feed on us, we live with them; there is no room
to choose
Between small feeders at the base and parasites at
loose.
Those lurching on like predators are wrecking earth
below,
Culling all its bounty, glutting on its seas,
Drawing on their neighbour, or sucking to appease.

Subjection we are under, servitude the state,
Domination seeks to rule us, we're caught as if by fate.
But safe from deep captivity in time we'll move
beyond;
One day we'll gladly serve again upon a distant shore -
In deference to one above, in deep dependency of love.

The cry of tin (an ingot of tin crackles when bent)

To make the tin and copper strong
They pillage from the rock within,
And some far knowledge draws them on
To forge that knife or sword of bronze.

Battle pours out, strength has won;
But on the screes and craggy ground
Humble tin is simply found.
Wet with Cornish rain it runs
Into moulds where open fires
Spit with ancient winter showers.

From the furnace and the fire,
Born of myth when all was quiet
Came the searing molten life
That donned the sword and deadly knife.

When the mixture's raised above,
Seeming axe with metal glove,
Little tin, its spirit meek, bends its head -
And cries for bed,
Within the rock where once it slept.

A Conceit

Never say a simple word,
Always convolute,
The meaning twists and twines a phrase
In its quest for truth.

With what giddy eyes, what strength,
The mistress can attract,
When on her bed she vexes
The poet's artful head.

And as he draws his little threads
And crafted metaphors,
They speak in words both suave to us,
And in his verse a quaint construct.

The mistress turns and tosses
Her raven tresses deep,
And he sees in their turning
A message, a conceit.

A flea jumps on, a flea jumps off,
The world is now within,
And with its blood it carries there
A symbol for our sin.

Not so Funereal

Sunflowers were the last lament
And such a one to make suns melt,
And molten hid behind grey skies
With hint of angels and goodbyes.
The bluebell haze had not appeared
When the deathly moment passed,
When the power of breath slow ceased
And one poor creature crept to peace.
Every mourner felt for her,
Knew the song was for her star,
And though we failed in many ways
To ease the life while here she stayed
We may hope that when she sees
The tributes paid and mourners grieve,
And future gently growing trees,
And meadow spread with new-born flowers
And children playing in the bowers;
She will favour us with prayers,
From the sunlit land now gained
Where we'll greet her once again;
Where eternity knows no pain.

October 2013

Grand Clichés

Sun, sky, earth, moon, stars and sea;
A commonplace in poesie;
Yet they remain a bedrock; vault;
A dream-house where our souls are caught –
By the ever-expanding sight,
Of naked day, and sacred night.

They are luminous and bright,
They are distant, touching near,
Shining, burning, gloating, high,
Gloomy, languid, ebbing slow,
Far surpassing what we know.

So they are most of what is fine –
So they are things that we declare;
We can't complain, bewail or cry
Without their sentiments so high.
We cannot gladness; sadness feel
Without gazing sun to sea -
The vaulted night and its pale gleam,
To glimpse infinity between.

They have become our virtual rock,
In whose crevice now we rest,
While overhead and down below,
Grand Clichés multiply and grow.

All that litters

Bottles, bags cans and rags, discarded underhand;
Commercial and domestic dross becomes a true
    wasteland.

Testimony to a trademark sham, a furtive spent
    expense,
Where the dirty harvest is cast and blown, not blessed.

All our spent possessions, unwanted daily bread,
Are tossed aside, forgotten, for others daily shed.

Streets are like to sewers with garbage on the ground,
While cats keep company with rats,
Scouring the unclean town.

A sense of proportion

Don't wallow in discomfort,
Save that for those in pain.

See the comic side of life,
See the clever side of jest.
For irony is seldom spent.

Thank God for just a black eye
And not a broken head.
For if it weren't so serious....
I wouldn't think on death.

Phobia

What strange fear grips the heart and head,
Is this real and never ends?

Down to places we would shun,
Even wonder of the sun.

Not indulging, feasting sad,
Nor a feature, being mad.

This is craving peace of mind,
This is fleeing without sound.

Apex Predator

Crouched upon some shining hill
The creature slouches down below
To feast upon the things we love;
Be they fine or be they just.

Be they rotten, or refined,
He will always be inclined
To break our peace if it exists
Or darken places and enlist

The worst of us to take his bid,
The sum of us to do his plan.

But see him falter, see him fail
A monster caught and stark unmanned,
Like some mere sprite in children's hands!

Able was I ere I saw Elba

Can it be both ways make sense
When we coin a word or phrase,
Looking, spelling just the same,
At beginning, through its length,
With a rhythmic consequence?

Is there any rhyme to this,
Is there reason lodged in sense,
Or is it all pure circumstance,
A plain, defined coincidence?

Names like Hannah, Anna, Eve,
Framed about when we're conceived;
Conjuring some imagery,
Reading with pure symmetry.

Does this forward, backward run,
Through the lexicon for fun?
Palindromes are quizzical,
And sometimes hard to find;
Unregarded as we pass
Aloof from page to page
Undermined as if they're just
Another feature lost to us.

Is such a word invented,
Does such a phrase expand? -
With little point in claiming
A strange preceding plan?

Fluency

Some struggle for words to stammer or say,
Awkward or gauche they splutter their way.

Yet they turn aside and see talking afresh,
Mouths like a flower pattering breath;
Ingress and egress, exuberance, power,
Easy of speech, exchanging for hours.

How is the nature born of the breath,
How can one fluency silence the rest?
And does the message that peoples express
Flow through the psyche as one that is deaf?

A special place

We all own a special place,
Some lifted up in worldly eyes
And lauded by society;
Others rested in their graves
Without a tribute, or a name.

We in time, like most, forget
The friends we met or friends now dead,
For here we only last as long
As faded memories or songs.

And the objects of the grave
Tarnish, fade or quite degrade.
There are some that live on most,
Those we hold to guard our soul.

Not though the sword from battle cry,
Nor the chattels, things of war;
Cruel men in arms abound,
But then stay firmly underground.
For nothing gainsays the final command.

Lost but found

She wandered hopelessly at night,
The owl kept watch and the moon was bright.
Below the canopy of stars
Something wanton dogged her path;

And through the ditches, in the rain,
Across wet logs, through thorns in pain,
The wretched, wronged and dismal girl,
Clung to hardened trees and grieved –
Life a wrack and nature's curse;
Injuries from man and worse.

Then a distant glow is seen;
Hopeless eyes glimpse gentle gleams,
And in the silence she espies
Doors that open, light inside;
Lit with candles and with fire;
Kindled warmth and lowly minds,
Genuine and unrefined.

On the walls white and bare,
No need to count, no clock was there.
But the crucifix just stared,
So they talked and dried her tears,
And the years rolled back, once free –
And they asked her back for tea.

The art of war

Whoever conceived the art of war?
Whoever defaced chivalric lore?

Were the knights even not as we dreamed?
Ravishing virgins and turbulent Queens?

We revelled in conquest,
Marvelled at guile,
Killed all our kinsmen
And murdered the child.

Whoever shouted (sword in hand)
That to honour the land is to defy
What we hear each day
from an orphan's cry? -

The pitiless host that stoke the fire;
While the mother's mourning
And the still birth raving
Grieves the angels' sky.

Ducks

They voyage diligently and swim differently;
With ease they tread the water's edge,
And tempt for their daily bread
With a petulant prayer.

Children flock to their waterside shrine,
The birds part-clumsy, part shining divine;
With often a thought to be preened and clean,
But sometimes to feast on that morsel of wheat.

And that's the repast we sometimes concede,
Leaving them lonely and dark in the weeds;
Where streams converge and slow currents flow,
And the voyagers huddle for comfort below.

Lovers they kiss and see them anew
Leaving the creatures, so faithful and true.

Bringing fire to the earth

Bringing fire to the earth was not a bad plan,
Planting division unleashed man for man
The freedom to love or to hate and despise
The bonds of our nature, the friendship that ties;
Broken then healed by the fervour divine.

But did we envisage those battlements set,
Families riven by civil unrest,
Just like inheritance left from the wars,
Just like the modern betrayal of accord?

Then as today was a difficult line,
Hard to accept, hard to define;
But certain to purify filth on the earth,
Fire needs to be kindled and flourish at first.

'I have come to bring fire on the earth, and how I wish it were already kindled'

Luke 12:49

The Thankful Villages

They were happy when greeted by bells,
The victors returned to the village still quiet,
Where the bombs never touched the birds in flight,
And the steeple kept watch over myriad skies.

Far upon distant expanse of fields
The villagers battled their fellows in blood,
As neighbours petitioned the powers above.

And something conspired to bring them all home,
Every last man (now etched on the stone),
Lodged in their graveyard where now they all rest,
For at the last hour God knows how, but they left.

The Great Persecution

Wash us white in flowing blood;
Contrary it seems to us;
Dress us in pure clothes divine;
Let us taste the last-served wine,
When in rows we stand and wait,
When we gaze and simply praise,
And raise all colours to the sky,
Where double rainbows hang so high;
And underneath their golden rays
Where little lambs and lions play,
See the white-robed tireless choir,
Tested by the burning fire,
Ever-onward, lost from time,
They are saints of yours and mine;
For they're the ones who suffered most
And earned their place amid the hosts.

Sleeping in the Lord

Sleep is prayer unbeknownst
And breathes a sigh when we're at rest,
To lighten moods in mornings fair
When we might wake, so glad we're there.

Still wrapped in dawn's unfolding day,
There we lie, and there we lay
When darkness intervened at night
With tempered dreams and some respite;

Curtains brightened in the glow
Leave us sad or filled with hope;
All our damage heals with time,
And love calls softly: 'friend of mine'.

Influences

There is an influence that grows,
Absorbed from nature's earth,
Or from the womb to educate
The moment's lively birth.

Given once the nurture,
Drawing knowledge from its bounds,
From the desert's barrenness,
Or child in comfort found.

Home or heath, church or moor,
The flow of change is there,
And though we thought we knew the way,
We knock at some strange door.

But there's a tainting in the air,
Behind the half-closed door,
A borrowed sense of runes once read,
Seeping everywhere.

The words we read, once fixed and set,
We lose the chance to say,
For hardly can we coin that phrase,
Or talk again in natural ways.

A leap of faith

Staring at the chasm he stepped,
And the gentle breeze gave no sense
Of thinkable death.

Some drifted birds tumbled in a clear sky,
While the snake was wary in its rock on high.

His heart leapt, and every dread
And every memory had,
Appeared for him in that place,
In the adrenalin-charged head.

He seemed a convict with his noose,
But carefully entwined and wrapped
Around the feet, elastic thread;
Not the sentence, not the neck.

Then birds like ravens sat just there,
Without a granary (he recalled),
And thus no need for nagging care.

And then that leap, and what a fall,
Flowers blossomed bright with bees;
Optical expanse unleashed –

Winds blew down and force increased;
But the sea sat silent with surcease.

Paper tigers and feeble dragons

Such is this where once I wrote,
Sentiments on paper notes;
But some who've written far before
Have turned the substance more to force;
Where paper's shown itself a shield,
For words reveal what strength conceals.

Nations hurtle, cities fall,
Still the enemy withdraws.
There to fight another day,
While we with flimsy show display.

Ps 9: 20 '… let the nations know that they are only human.'

A face too far

My mind is fixed but broken, scattered on the wing
Of butterflies and spirits, and all created things.

My body aches and trembles as if with parting touch,
Without the healing fabric no language is enough.

My eyes are simply clarified since I began to weep,
Released to mourn death's scourges, and rest within
her sleep.

But most of all my heart has left and fled without a
trace,
To dwell upon the lustre of her uplifted face.

Praise

Sweet noise that from the mouth of her
Runs swiftly on the flow
Of river drenched in evening's bliss,
Deep Waveney down below:
Where dragonflies, black messengers
Alight with swift, brief lives
And settle in a moment's breeze,
So delicate and light.

Her gentle mouth, like water's source,
Pours forth abundant praise,
White garment matched by darkness
Amid the sun's last rays.
With arms outstretched to praise her Lord
Her music fills the air.
And we are drawn to worship
In the fragrance fair.

The fading evening draws its breath
About the fields of thyme
And we are lonely wanderers
In a peaceful clime.
And then to fellowship unknown,
The birds sing on till dark;
We walk the damp grass back to home,
Brief friendship; hopes that last.

July 2014

Gentleness

Have a heart to be broken,
    to be mended with a kiss.
Find the betrayer among you,
    and kill him with tenderness.
Never the rash condemnation;
Never the violent mind;
Always the peace be upon you,
    through your eyes let the gentleness shine.
The spirit is poor and emptied,
    but then we are fearsome and strong.
And to live unconfined, is to live as a child,
    Renouncing all things that are wrong.

July 2014

Ice and Fire

When tundra turned to prairie
And sunflowers bloomed far north,
With petals and wet forests
Claimed the ice with warmth.

The faint sun flickered tar-pits,
Tombs of those that ran,
The frost-encrusted fierce ones,
Tigers, wolves and lions,
Trapped now within quaint spaces
For wonderment inside;
Beside the woolly mammoth,
Magnificent in death,
Whose shroud of flowers and insects
Once wrapped him with their breath.

They once envisaged granite peaks,
Where green trees wax and wane,
Millennia of conifers,
First here, now there again,
Drifting with the movement
Of life in constant flow;
The lunge of melting waters
With creatures they let go –
Megafauna washed ashore,
Fossilled fangs and teeth,

Lost ones slowly turned to dust
Beneath the slow retreat.

Beneath the sun came searing storms,
And fire begun by man –
For fire and foment was his game,
And killing was his plan.
The beasts knelt low, the land was purged
And there the bison fell,
Last remnant of the double blow,
Or man's swift overkill.

With guns he must accomplish
What nature long divines –
He rid the world of nuisance,
Oblivious of time -
And then he fixed his gun on us,
On you, on yours, on mine.

Gift or threat?

The missionary sees through the eyes
To glimpse the soul within;
Eyes of every hue and shade are seen as nothing then -
Only invitations, to find a hidden friend.

They try to walk in friendship,
We struggle on the shore –
Downcast by fear and loneliness,
Togetherness no more.

Eyes of light and dark and blue,
Together they would blend;
But we're accursed, we walk in night,
Fighting to the end:
There's a challenge in that look;
A callous threat that stares;
If only love could conquer
And call a heart to care.

But can we even trust our own,
Or promise to ourselves?
We seem to walk with sideways glance -
Scared of vague reflections
Dimly in that glass.

What a curiosity indeed:
A planet of disaster,
Riven by a flood and tide
That none can truly master.

Fear itself

When times turn sour and thoughts turn grim,
Darkened by death and its blackened wings;
Then we grimace in dismay
For strength has failed with industry,
Or its bankrupt friend economy.

Then the fear on fear it grows,
And multiplies from man to man,
Till the great Colossus stands
On ravaged, barren, empty land.

The men, morose on vacant streets
Wait for news that never comes,
Brood with dreams that soon are lost,
Count on hope that springs each day
Crushed and fallen, falls away.

Impotence in all its turns
Curses manhood, curses lives;
Breeds discontent in lonely wives.
In a home where nothing grows
Is there such a thing as hope?

But they are told there's none to fear,
Nothing but that fear of fear -
Try telling that to those in dread
When they are railing in their beds.

Destruction of a dream

All around the trees are felled;
They break their backs and discord reigns,
Dismantled in a gentle place.
The incense and the fire abounds,
Like a torture thereabouts -

And creatures dumb are burnt alive,
Or run amok to salvage lives.
And the place for which they strive,
From the wreckage that they flee,
Is not the paradise we crave,
But simple earthly harmony.

Little chance have they or we
In such a brutal company;
Where progress is a worldly sum –
And heaven a clearing in the sun.

Then the clearings fast expand,
No more a space, but drifts of land;
Becoming masses of decline
Within the reckless human mind.

'Paradise is our native land' *St Cyprian*

Paradise

Everything you want awaits you there,
Things you've only dreamt of here below.
From a child we know the path to go;
Being good will lead to pure delight,
But does it tempt and tantalize our minds?

Whether furious or meek makes little sense,
The purpose is to act, and having lost all fear
They at once envisage their own deed.
We search for them, but they cannot be seen.

So one time another victim bled;
Now a host of innocents are dead;
And many from a void on earth now go,
Caught up before in chaos here below.

Does a paradise await us sweetly there,
Or does the flaming abyss search and tear?
We can only guess the last decree,
And quake at every horror that we see.

And then with fear and trembling turn away;
Hoping for a land where sense is free;
Not a sensual pleasure for our souls,
For such the land of mercy cannot be.

Time and travel

Speed harkens to its own thrill,
An idea of advancing as fast as any light
To the time that we are losing,
And the future just in sight.

A future never witnessed by our clay-bound, tardy
past,
And a future needing energy to capture and to pass.

A glimpse of super-nova flashing in the sky;
Apocalyptic nightmare in the blinking of an eye –
Such could be the glimpses of our future-frenzied
speed.

But is it worth an accident to find the love we seek,
To uncover love's new secrets,
Descendants we might meet –
To talk of Earth's disasters
Or impress them with our speed?

Childhood

Coming up from that warm hearth
Into life's shrewd smiles and stares;
From a house or steaming slum,
Where love was shared, or no one cared.

And in the emanating stream
Of childhood threats and latent dreams,
Someone forlorn, lost is born,
Whose promise is a boat in storm.

Which destination, harbour blessed?
Which embarkation leads to rest?
The sea can never, never rest,
Its moon is pulling every tide –

In its waves move shifting stones
Where all our children swim alone.

Friendship

More than any pearl enclosed so deep,
Far beyond the reach of angry nets,
Substance of the one and other bound,
In acceptance and in trust once found.

More than any tall, unconquered peak,
Radiated by the sun, beyond, above,
Is the touch of friendship warmed by love,
Is the spell of language from the heart.

More than any mansion, save the many,
Or the game that builds for fame or money,
Stands the bond that calls to live together,
Now for just a day, but then forever.

The dunes

Through the sand dunes waving grass in constant sun,
We plough with feet soft-slipping every one;
The harshness and the dryness of the marram,
The landscape fine and ancient, calmly barren.

On to paths through meadows in the heat,
Beyond the silent sea past shining beach,
We tread towards the pine trees and the lake,
Where boats are moored, their wood on water bright;
Moving with the rhythm of the sea,
Yet trapped like toys in sheltered estuary.

So we pass flotillas in the mind,
Ever onwards down the paths we glide;
Pine cones scattered as we duly step,
Needles at our arms, and feet where they are shed.

Sunlight enters softly through the trees,
Glances at us briefly then is lost;
Squirrels scamper faintly up above,
When the clearing rings with bird-song sweet,
And we find the fallen pines to rest our feet.

Moving on

We wait for new adventure,
A keener appetite,
Unbounded in the outlook,
No sense in looking back.
Ground once lost no object;
There's nothing we can lack.

And in the transformation,
The passage moving on,
We travel dark, imperfectly,
From city, town to town.
From country street to country lane,
From house to house we find,
Security is not a place,
But vision is the ground.

Surroundings clear, a simple taste
For every changing year,
Companions to share food with us,
And voice their hopes and fears.

Until our voices falter,
Just like a moment's breath,
Until the earth is held quite still
Beyond those heights and depths.

And then our wandering life is past,
The silence falls and fills
And all our moving spirits pass,
And peace perfects the will at last.

Estimation

No sense in hurling diatribes
When others' lives you doubt,
No sense in sinking to despise
When others' lives you hate –
Your ideas and fears
Embroil a troubled mind;
Your hatred and anxiety
Scroll like sand and water
In adversity.

Only time will wear the two in one,
Unless the hand of friendship shakes not shuns.
Then the eyes, those beacons of the soul,
Must become accompanists to song;
Songs our lonely ones to chorus blending,
Quivering notes from old, or young, and strong.

For only then will discord be discarded,
Harmony restored and faith united,
Trust unveiled, protection granted;
From our own entangled spite and degradation;

Waiting for that judge of clear-cut arbitration,
Who calls the tune of every estimation.

A New Season

Not heralded by stars and promise bright,
But with grey skies and sodden black of night;
Colourless the nature of its day
Where a blackbird stands all wet with rain;
Apparition of the garden, sole survivor,
But in the boles of trees there life endures
And shifting under leaves, the seasons' years.

Light and dark

Beyond there lies some firmament vastly washed with
tears,
Of light from every galaxy and fall-out from the wars.

There they only harken and stare with deep regret
Upon the course of ages and all our dark distress.

For they can see our ruin from some land far away
Where noon and night which trouble us are just one
timeless day;

Where light is not an answer to darkness or a threat,
But gently a reminder of tidings that we lack.

Photographs

Passages of time we cut them short,
Collected and implanted in the mind
From days gone past.

Now a vinyl overcoat for memories
And happiness we felt,
A thought caught in advance,
A glance or look
Once troubled or inclined,
Under glass now watching,
Solitary-confined.

Staring from the wall they reassure,
That sentimental smile still warm and bright,
Now staring from the dead with abundant life.

How curious to share this intimacy;
These black and white
So clear as if from yesterday.
Then colour cuts a new contrast in red and white,
Clothes blossom like the flowers known in life;
And many images their fondness glows,
And all is captured,
All is plucked and all is borrowed,
For the future time and for tomorrow.

Meanings

Do you sense a meaning in our world,
Like the meaning of a word its vortex turns,
Its provenance both deep and overrun,
Fraught with conflict, warped by trade,
Subject to the wars and seas' advance,
Coined by emperors and kings
With a human and almighty face.

How did we manage to exist,
Under each and every existential threat,
How survive to tell our tale
In provincial language that we know,
In the library where some truth is lodged,
In dictionaries that tell us part of who we are
Or in manuscripts that move and slowly grow?

The Donkey and the horse

What meandering creature makes its way,
Humbly, gently, meekly, up from Galilee?
It was the mount of solemn, holy kings,
And now to beat of tambours, crowds and angels sing.

Summoned by the master, loosened from his bonds,
Now the creature breathes and pants with joy,
Unlimited this journey to on high,
Unprompted does the donkey gladly ride.

Hosanna turns the darkness into light,
With palms and garments scattered from above,
And decadence now turns its head to love.

But round about the horses toss their heads,
Their garments leather and their brazen necks.
Bit and harness clamp with glinting power
While soldiers with their helmets rue the hour.

Metal and steel rattle their tune,
But for the Victor's death is the mystery tomb.

Reflected Glory

The moon's pure bluish light
Tries its best to incandesce
And runs its languid course;
Strength of memory and remorse -
Overrun by the sun
And its sure cosmic force.

Think of all our borrowed glory,
Crowns, tiaras, robes of state,
Or the stature that we're craving
When we try to emulate.

Try to prove who's best,
And with a little greatness you might shine;
But Glory is a higher thing;
A robe and dress divine.

Healing

Healing has for many gone,
It's now a modern science;
With reason as the backbone
And the body as a platform.

Tested, laid on tables, cut - precision now,
Laser and mechanics make you wonder how
The surgeon has this sureness, to treat our inner self,
To even enter consciousness, and seem to cut it out.

They are marvels of assurance,
Far more since basic times,
When trades took on the measure
Of healing us inside.

But from the mind illusion grows,
Confusion through those nerves:
With altered states we seem; we are,
Transmitting nowhere, but afar.

Impedimenta

We struggle through the battlefield,
Or scramble down a hill,
Laden down with armaments,
Beset by missiles shrill.
It's exquisite agony to carry such a load,
The body has its own dead weight,
Without a further curse.

Strength can be a substitute,
But this will soon be spent;
Stamina has certain power,
But falters in the end.
At length the strong arm fails us,
The weakness in our breast;
Weighed down by rampant gravity,
We lose our parting breath.

There was a bond from man to man;
Our comrades helped us cope,
But we can labour vainly
Without the lightness of a yoke;
The one that's laid upon us
So we can have some rest;
We know the anguish borne before
By one with higher strength.

On the way

There is a deep significance
To roads and vital tracks,
Our passages through times before,
And steps to call us back.

Now we speed along them,
Then we wandered lame,
But our destination
Is more or less the same.

Some place of spotless sanctity,
Some river running deep,
Where we might wash our sins away
Or find a cure for sleep.
We're restless till we're moving,
We must be moving on -
There it is a meaning,
As we speed or crawl along.

The men on motorbikes they push –
Against the flight of time;
They shimmer in the distance,
Black specks like insect lives.

And animals in stately rows,
Migrating on their way;
Camels and their caravans
Trek on till break of day.

The roads are long and dangerous,
The narrow paths they wind;
But we often meet a stranger
On a certain way we find.

And there they met a stranger,
Who told them all they knew,
Who seemed a touch familiar,
Whose influence just grew.
They wondered at the way he spoke,
As they walked along;
But it was only once he parted
And left them unaware
That they recognized the roadway
And the face they gazed on there.

Tendentiousness

It is a great temptation to write the way we speak,
To put across an argument, to seem as if we teach.

A due impartiality, is that the gift to have,
To tender observations and leave it just at that?

It would be self-defeating though to only speak in
turn,
For such as words of beauty have a power of their
own.

When we write about a life, it then becomes our own,
When we describe a living thing we give it then a
home.

Can we isolate it then, to live without a claim? -
As we discuss its basis when we love or write its name

There, we make a judgment if it's wonderful in verse,
Even if it's only of very humble birth;

And all its sweet environs and every part we see
Are cloaked in images and phrase, but part of history.

A story that's unfolding like a bud that brings life on,
Has it an origin to praise, in verse, or rhyme or song?

So beauty and its truth, enough (that sweet elusive
  blend),
Steeped in all traditions, tendentious to the end.

Peace amid thorns

More from the hereafter;
Not such for being here.
Their look is to the future,
But while they fix their stare,
And gently or remotely
Touch our feelings as we haste,
Or settle our own appetite
Which hungers for the chase –

They rest with solemn countenance
(but maybe not quite that)
For not like us unhappy,
Or miserable or sad.
They are not spectators,
But witnesses right here
As all the promise of the world
They must recount and bear.

It is sheltered in their footsteps,
Broken as they care,
While they are calm amid the thorns
Of turmoil and despair.

Thinking of our worldly shame,
They still have eyes for us;
A smile perhaps is out of place,
But hinted at in part;

And they continue praying
For a simple change of heart.

Solemnity it seldom smiles,
But when it does it gleams,
For something truly joyful
Has touched a soul that's truly free.

Spoiling for a fight

We're eager to confront a foe; aggression seems
 creation;
But where is peace among the games enlisting our
 attention?

We're baffled by the lonely cry of 'cease' that goes
 unheeded –
As we prepare for rampage, it really is unneeded.

Perhaps you could take cover, or suffer all you like:
We really have gone further than spoiling for a fight.

Old Boy Network

Is there reassurance about a nob or toff?
They sit there with position,
They sit there with the cash;
And somehow they can seem relaxed,
And liberal at that.

Are they the quintessential snobs
With a rosy nose?
Brought up on port and oranges
Or decked in ermine robes?

No doubt they are still tender,
Underneath a front,
And just like us they suffer
From the world's affront.

They may be often hated;
They represent a class,
But if they sink to hating
Then appearance turns to farce.

When they sit in parliament,
So cosy and so close;
There is a bond between them,
Elitist to the last.

But to be elitist
Is to look on something high
And with some wise compassion
Could make for something fine.

A dog to stay

Don't worry -
When you were away
I had good company.
Your dog he never asked for much,
Just sat patiently;
And when we went for walks,
(apart from getting very wet),
He didn't trouble me.

I hardly gave him any treats,
Hardly anything;
A drink of water on and off,
A morsel in his tin.

A couple of cheesy biscuits,
His meagre rations then to eat;
A big fat juicy butcher's bone
And half a joint of meat...

Birds

Birds are free,
But always find their roost,
Flying through a dappled sunlit sky.

Morning, evening have no hold on truth
While the hues and meanings flood the mind.
Withheld, yet unrestrained, the drama flies
And in the night observant they reside.

Clothed they are and fed those birds of light,
Without a hindrance, quick and soft and bright;
And we, as they, might travel far afield
If we take on as joyfulness our shield –

Returning to a home as to a nest;
Finding pure adventure
And sweet rest.

Bonfire of the Vanities

Everything goes up in smoke,
Incense offered gladly;
No mercy for the lust for life:
A god of hate and anger.

With the mirror on the wall,
And ones who look on vainly
Destroy and burn all that is new,
All luxury, all finery.
While wantonness in idle dress
Provokes a bigot's fury.

When all settles
Into dust and ashes, and is over,
The pain of losing what we love
(or all our misdemeanours),
The vanity of who we are,
(our follies and endeavours),
Become as nothing in exchange
For resurrected freedom,
Emerging from the darkness
And fear of brief destruction.

For all our vanities are freed,
We look upon the mirror;
In modern times we see ourselves,
And glass lives on forever.

And wherever thought was spurned,
Its substance simply widens;
For fires consume but not destroy
What they seek to silence.

Live and let live

Mottled are the colours that can make us yearn
When mixed with every pigment from the brush;

For they become emotion-charged as we discern
Each rainbow-sheltered fragment that we touch.

Leave the birds to their own nest; each swallow let it
fly,
Go lark, aspire, ascending, fervently on high.

Release the bird within your hand and open up the
sky;
Tomorrow it could drift, and fall emotionless to
ground;

And what a waste of wonderment, to see it waste a day;
An ornament that's broken, and never found its way.

SBNR

I'm very spiritual and kind, but really not religious –
Is this a contradiction once for all, or is that just
ridiculous?
I'm sure I'm fine to be detached and remain in general,
general;
When I meet another I may seem then more natural.

It makes a deal of difference if we're spiritually-
inclined,
But not to lavish hope with trust or make a false
appearance –
To seek a leader of a kind;
For the world is my adherence.

To have denomination could be a social curse,
To ignore all those impressions, and those who love
the world –
The beauty of the sun and moon and walks along the
beach,
A longing for the foreign shore, and gently-swaying
trees.

So I'll remain quite neutral, and natural I've become,
To meditate is all it takes, or run, and run, and run…
I'd rather cherish woodland trees (and find a partner
with some ease),

Than spend a sorry lifetime searching vainly on my
knees.

Scribes to help us write

A scribe deciphers what they think
From what they vaguely say;
They may not have an argument
And may not well explain
What they only feel inside
And learn from day to day.

It is an understood event,
We understand their plight,
Were they not involved enough
Or set to read or write?
And it's not a simple task
To express or grasp a thought,

When thoughts have little symmetry
And questions often asked
Explore within a consciousness
And pull apart our past.

Such a talent to be lost,
Such promise still interred;
When language fails,
Its consequence
Is something without words.

To spare a hare

Confused by roaming headlights it hesitates in fright,
And all its vain manoeuvres and movements in and out
Only multiply the danger of collision in the night.

I feel anticipation in braking to remove
An agony of heartbreak, swelling as I move.
And some relief spills over as we still share the world,
One driving now quite chastened,
One resting near the kerb.

There is a brief contentment,
A peace comes somehow there,
Now that the creature passes by
And I have spared a hare.

The Great Exchange

Strange place for any virgin, discovering her lot,
Amid the shame of poverty, the smell of things that
rot.
Not a hareem palace, nor a vestal's fire alight,
But instead a 'prayer accepted' by a purely spotless
mind.

Eternal sunshine promised, by a poet of the past,
Is at best discovered in some memory that lasts;
Recollection of a time gone by, a scene where all was
new,
Which can become our present here, a paradise to
view.

We rid our minds of poison, and damage there within,
To look instead on gentle peace and every humble
thing –
And notice in obscurity the earth remains so clean,
And there within a stable true majesty is seen.

We cannot now embellish this unlikely, simple home,
For in its very essence is a grandeur of its own.

'How happy is the blameless vestal's lot!
The world forgetting, by the world forgot.
Eternal sunshine of the spotless mind!
Each pray'r accepted and each wish resign'd'

Alexander Pope

Not just social?

We come from friendly animals,
We mix in every class,
A stable, humane, social world,
Is not a lot to ask.

We haven't got a dignity,
Innate or given free,
And every war that's ever fought
Is for a deity –
One that drives us to the wall,
With violence to regret,
While evermore our spark of life
Is something deep inbred –
Received from those ancestors,
Developed from our past,
Descending to those creatures,
Not implanted in the heart.

To build a harmony on Earth
Should not be untoward,
After all the wars will pass,
Enlightenment will dawn;
No beating swords to ploughshares –
That will all be done.
For man will lay his own sword down,
And peace will surely come;
And at the church and altar,

Reason takes the pew;
Where a cast of human strangers
Is the family we view.

Accidents

Is it mere appearance this accident we see,
Or is it more substantial, not simply red or green,
And there within the fabric is reality unseen?

Even mere appearance is the fact that strikes us most,
Draws us to a principle (that could be the first);
For red or blue or roundness, they never seem inert;
They have a value and a power; emotion, passion,
    worth.

To some it is pure energy, to others form is dead;
Appearance may be just a word, like simple daily
    'bread'.

Solomon's promise

King of great repute,
A man more like a god,
Building temples, raising arms,
His forces massed in line;
Within, the wives that called his name;
A mass of concubines.

More to a man than wealth or fame –
He made a just reply;
When asked what was the noble path,
He chose an understanding heart.

But all can slip into decay;
Even wisdom masks a flaw;
Promise that's forever bright
Is not forever sure.

When faith and superstition
Were agents of the age,
Integrity – Idolatry
Made shocking counter-claims.

Somnambulists

Upon the stairs or kitchen floor
They gaze it seems quite blind;
No expression troubles them –
A vacancy of mind.

They were in bed some time ago,
But now they wander free,
Or remain quite motionless -
Unaware of you or me.

Was there a clock that stirred them,
That prompted them to stray?
Or was it some vague fear or fright,
Below the threshold in the night?

But there's no trepidation,
As they shift from room to room,
No fear of wild intrusion,
For they are roaming free;

Just walking blind about the world -
Somehow like you or me.

The Tripod

There is a mass, a strength in three,
A structure with dimension;
An equal bearing of the weight,
Combined with real intention.
To understand or comprehend:
To learn and pray and love
Are like the furniture of life
We cannot sense enough.
And when we seek to be sustained
By sure stability,
There is no further help or aid
Than found in just these three.

Cf. St Benedict – a balance between work, prayer and rest.

Doctor

There must be more to this poor body spare;
Please understand and guide me through this land.

Without a prejudice I trust you –
Find the beatings of my heart;
Without a sense of jaundice –
Seek the structures where they lurk:
The secret throngs of enemies
That flourish in the depth;
Our witnesses or alibis,
In length or breadth or breath.

From the utmost principle
That leads us to your door –
Not what you enter in to us,
But what proceeds before.
Not the imperfection of joint or bone or limb,
Nor the pervious system
Whose weakness sighs within.

But that which you explore with us,
You ask us to become;
Reveal the inner matter,
Lead from hail to sun.

Nothing is just piety,
Nothing proud or feigned;
Be scientist or pharmacist,
With wisdom of the sage.

Our hearts resume their working beat;
A privilege we cry,
And the mind that's overwhelmed
Presents a soulful, tearful eye.
We don't demand an answer;
But we offer what we can –
So, doctor, teach us something –
Learn to understand.

Enquirers

A fellow human being,
To explore our unsolved past
And future ever present,
You draw a veil so fast
Upon the tracery of stars
That pin the world to sight,
Beyond the undercurrent
Of ever-moving light.

You penetrate a galaxy
As it unfolds with haste
Or try with quiet patience
The maker's silent face.
With calm perceptive reason
You claim to find some truth;
But more like divination
Your thesis lacks a proof.

What if unknown planets
Burst or wildly spin,
Or depths of sounding water
Gush from silken rain;
What if thoughts of marvel,
Cosmic sky or clime
Create a wave of feebleness
Or chaos in our time?

Then you've made a thesis,
A step for humankind;
For then you know how theory
Could unbalance every mind.

Love

To hold a baby seems like love,
But may be more like fear.
To hold a woman could be love;
But is it just she's near?
Let's uncover what this love is,
Let's define, declare;
But we only sense a feeling,
And one that's hard to share.

Then there are the bridges,
Burnt or crossed to bear -
Can we believe in others
And does it pay to dare?
And love must be a paying love
Not a game or toy,
So is affection tested,
Do we confront our joy?

And who are we to claim to love
When little aid we give
To those we owe the benefit,
To those for whom we live?
Is there a consolation in finding
Others care, when we can only
Steal a heart,
Not take our cross to bear?

Time will test intentions
And while there's time we must
Win or lose this shadow game,
We all play upon this earth.
It's harder though to fathom
The look in one fair face
Than to contemplate the mystery
That permeates this place.

Somewhere

Somewhere upon the meadow lands
There is a place that's free;
Banished from the memories
And aching of the heart –
A place where trees and plants and flowers,
In air as free as ice is bound,
Sway beneath the mountain sides
With sunshine all around.

It makes the colour brighter
And air is fresh and clean;
Somehow white seems crystal,
The sky directs its gleam.
The very earth cannot be seen,
It is all varied shades of green –
And through it all run breezes,
From a place unseen.

It is still there this other place,
A long way off from here
Worth more than we will ever know,
A thing we need not fear.
It's good to recollect this hope,
Somewhere we've never seen,
In case our emptiness at home
Becomes our only dream.

ND - #0262 - 080726 - C0 - 197/132/8 - PB - 9781784562670 - Matt Lamination